LAWS OF LIFE

LAWS OF LIFE

Donna Duffield

LAWS OF LIFE

iUniverse books may be ordered through booksellers or by contacting:

iUniverse
1663 Liberty Drive
Bloomington, IN 47403
www.iuniverse.com
1-800-Authors (1-800-288-4677)

Because of the dynamic nature of the Internet, any web addresses or links contained in this book may have changed since publication and may no longer be valid. The views expressed in this work are solely those of the author and do not necessarily reflect the views of the publisher, and the publisher hereby disclaims any responsibility for them.

Any people depicted in stock imagery provided by Thinkstock are models, and such images are being used for illustrative purposes only. Certain stock imagery © Thinkstock.

ISBN: 978-1-5320-0048-5 (sc)
ISBN: 978-1-5320-0050-8 (hc)
ISBN: 978-1-5320-0049-2 (e)

Library of Congress Control Number: 2016910072

Print information available on the last page.

iUniverse rev. date: 12/08/2016

BIOGRAPHY

My childhood was a difficult one with a variety of different experiences that rendered me when I left home, at 16yrs, extremely dysfunctional. I had so many issues within and without I would have been a psychiatrist dream. At the age of 21yrs I simply did not want to live anymore; I had done nothing but suffer and I had no reason to believe my future was going to be any different. I had gone to many professionals but they were unable to help me. I suffered with depression, anxiety, fear, paranoia, drug, alcohol and food addictions. I was bulimic and anorexic and could not hold down a job for more than a few months. I had no qualifications and no parental support. I was on my own and completely lost. One day as I was walking through the streets of London, completely desperate and alone, I came to the realization that I did have a choice. I could kill myself. After realizing that I felt somewhat relieved that at least I had a way to make the suffering end. However, I decided that before I did that I must at least give myself the chance at finding out why I was suffering so much. That was the beginning of my journey and it eventually led me to questioning my own existence and the existence of God.

Every day I searched and contemplated these questions, every day I looked within myself and found some form of delusional thought pattern and emotional turmoil. I watched and watched for years until what seemed like a constant awareness arose whereby I had no choice but to watch. From this came knowledge that set me free. My depression eventually stopped, as did my anxiety, fear and addictions. One by one, year after year, my suffering became less. At the age of 34yrs I began giving talks and writing. Prior to that I had managed to complete two degrees in the area of Psychology. Now I run the Laws of Life workshops which in a nutshell consists of all the wisdom that I have gained over the years and all the laws that eventually set me free from suffering.

I believe we all have the right to live without constant suffering but nothing and no one can save you from that but yourself. My desire is not to force my ideas on anyone; my desire is only to share what I learnt along the way.

Who is Donna Duffield?

Am I my faults?

I can be a know it all
I can be insecure in relationships
I can be critical when I see something wrong
I can find listening hard when I am emotional
I can be selfish with the remote control
I can be a perfectionist
I can be straight to the point of being perceived as rude
I can get angry
I can be a drama queen

My good points?

I would do anything for anyone without reward
I may be critical but I'm not judging
I continually look at myself to transcend my faults
I am straight so you can trust me
I love everyone I meet without exception
I love nature and look after it
I take nothing personal even when hurt
I do not hate anyone
My intentions are always to do good because I care
I let go of anger very quickly
I take my lead from God always

Who am I?

These are just character traits, personality and conditioning;
they change constantly and thus can't be ME.

I am love trapped in the body of mind,
emotions and conditioning;
To know me you must 'feel' me
To feel me you must feel yourself
To feel yourself you must understand yourself

We are perfect in being, flawed in personality.
When suffering rises it is a sure sign it's that time
again to look within and understand.
Each time you do that you feel the essence of love as
your natural state becomes much deeper than before.

DEDICATION....

I've achieved many things
Lived many dreams
Had thousands of happy moments

But being a mum tops it all.

Thank you to Ella and Elliott for being
my greatest gift in this life.

Mum x

INTRODUCTION

Life is made up of simple but divine laws
Follow the laws and life will work for you in miraculous ways
Disobey the laws and life will seem like constant struggle

All men are equal under the law
There is no good and bad
Only truth and ignorance

Those that know the law will know peace and behave as such
Those that are ignorant to the law will
know suffering and behave as such

The purpose of existence is to know the law
Life is always trying to show you this everyday
If only you could read the signs

Many teachers have come to show the signs
I am one of them

It is not enough however to believe a teacher
Their job is only to show you
For the law to work you must apply it

The divine quality of following the law
It will set you free from suffering

GOD AND RELIGION

Some followers of religion get so caught up with following their religion

They forget God

 1

JUDGMENT

If you judge yourself
You will have no love
To love others

Non-Judgment starts with you first

Freedom from judgment
Comes with understanding....
Why you do what you do
Then you know why others do as they do

We behave bad because we feel bad
Not because we are bad
Knowing this brings compassion
Compassion transforms bad to good

OLD HABITS DIE HARD...

Let your heart decide
What's right for you
Not the people around You

Caring too much about what people think
Is an old habit
That destroys the freedom
To be as you are
And live the life you want

When your time Is up
Will you wish you had of pleased more people?
Or had the courage to please yourself?

INNER PEACE...

All we want in life is peace!

Without peace we cannot feel love
Without peace we cannot see beauty
Without peace we cannot be content

Peace comes not from changing all that surrounds you
It comes from changing that which is within you

Self-condemnation breeds guilt and destroys peace
Understanding breeds compassion and creates peace

Where are you?
In peace or conflict?

HABITS

Do you feel stuck - going round in circles?
Do you keep suffering with the same -
Pain, condition, situation or person?

You may see the truth
But yet it continues...?

Old habits die hard my friend
Some are as old as your birth
But many are from generations before
Put unto you to resolve
Too difficult for them to face

See the situation clearly
Go into it deeply
See your ignorance - more than theirs
Do not run - face yourself
The truth will eventually set you free

More than anything else
Be kind to yourself
This takes great courage

COMPASSION

You are doing the best you can...

Do you continue to fall?
You are supposed to.....
That's how we learn

No one is born perfect

Our greatest teachers faced internal battles
They too fell many times

Great teachers...
Get back up
Feel no pity
And no guilt

To get back up and grow
You must understand that you are destined to fall
To get back up and grow
You must know - life is tough!

Bigger Picture

If you think about the particulars of your life
You will find problems and suffering

If you think about why you are here
You will find, mystery, beauty, truth and God

What do you think about?

HEAVEN IS WITHIN YOU....

But you have to go through hell first, to get there
Hell is all of your conditioning, past pain, ignorance and ego

Let all your situations reveal to you your ignorance
And all that you have been searching for.....

Will be revealed!

LIFE'S GREATEST GIFT

Lessons are life's greatest gift....
They teach wisdom

Without wisdom there is no....
Peace, compassion, contentment and joy

The biggest gift wisdom taught me was....
Living without fear of the future
And guilt of the past

Without wisdom life was not worth living

Wisdom comes from your life situations
Particularly painful ones
You are not a victim of life
You are a student of existence

Look, listen and learn
And life will reveal its beautiful mystery

The True Meaning
Of Karma....

Doing something good
Does not create good karma
Unless it is done without....

'The desire to gain'

Doing something bad
Does not create bad karma
Unless it is done with....

'The intent to harm'

Karma is your internal energy
Manifesting everyday as your life circumstances
If you hold and create anger energy
You will create destructive circumstances
If you hold and create peaceful energy
You will create harmonious circumstances

You have to attract according to
Your internal energy
Past and what you create now with your mind

This isn't punishment
Its divine evolution
Karma is your mirror
You can only change that which you can see

YOUR SUFFERING IS
YOUR TEACHING...

Whatever you resist - persists!
Why?
Because in resistance to the situation
You also resist the teaching

You cannot by pass your divine destiny to learn
Without learning the human race could not exist

The rule is this....
As you change from within your life changes from without
Thus before you seek to change a painful situation
Seek to understand its teaching
If you change the situation before learning
The situation will simply repeat itself

Are you going round in circles?

Understand Suffering

To pass through the grips of suffering......
You must understand.....

Suffering comes from within
Not without

Circumstances are bringing your past pain to conscious awareness
Not causing it

Hidden in this pain
Is wisdom, depth, joy and divine connection

But....

First you must understand your suffering
Or....
You simply make more of it

Suffering Is Oxygen

At certain stages of your evolutionary growth
Suffering is as vital as oxygen

Without it you are....
Shallow, ignorant, a coward, blind, selfish and most of all without
knowledge of the divine Nature of life

You are here on earth to learn
When You Realize This, Your Suffering becomes your greatest gift

And your key to the greatest joy you have ever known

SUFFERING IS YOUR DIVINE GIFT

Freedom from suffering is in understanding suffering
Your greatest lessons are always in your greatest pain

Freedom from suffering is knowing how to deal with suffering
Understand, accept, feel and let go

Our greatest teachers, Jesus, Buddha, Gandhi, Nelson Mandela etc
Have often suffered the greatest pain
Their suffering was their teaching

Now It's our turn and mine
What is the teaching hidden in your suffering?
Do you know how to access it?
What are your circumstances trying to tell you?

When you know this your suffering will pass
Leaving only wisdom behind

Evolving Pains

Only when your suffering Is acute
Are you close to dissolving it
This is the process of evolving

To evolve you need experience and knowledge
Suffering will naturally attract your experience
And the sincere desire to see the truth
Will attract the right knowledge

Not Mad or Bad

You suffer not because you are mad, bad or guilty
You suffer because its your time to grow

Belief in God or not makes no difference
To be happy, at peace and content
Man has to evolve out of this stage of ignorance

If you suffer consistently with….

Anger, hatred, jealousy, insecurity, fear, anxiety, depression and addictions -

Then you are in the stage of growth not insanity

DESIRE IS GROWTH

Desire is an essential part of mans spiritual growth....

All desire is only man searching
To quench the relentless thirst for contentment

Such contentment cannot be found in the world
Only in returning back to his divine nature

Man must first search the world, however
In the form of his desires

When he satisfies all desire and still feels empty
Then he is ready to go in search
Of the divine

Thus...
Leave man to his desires
He must see the truth for himself

 17

Peace Starts With You

Man who is not at war within himself
Will not be at war outside himself

To create peace
You must first be at peace with yourself

To love another
You must feel love for within yourself

To stop judging another
You must first accept yourself

Self-condemnation for any reason
Creates anger and pain within War against the self
And conflict with another

18

STOP RUNNING

Alcohol, drugs, cigarettes,
Food, sex, gambling, masturbation etc....

Regardless of your addiction type
All can be transcended with true understanding

Your compulsion to obsessively engage in any behavior
Without the ability to stop - is an addiction

In truth however it is your body and mind trying
To tell you something important
But you are not listening
You are running

You are running from
Emptiness, boredom, pain, problems, stress

Stop running
And your addictions will stop too

A Quiet Mind

When you quiet the mind
Suffering is not painful
It is felt as a little discomfort in the stomach

When you quiet the mind
Difficult situations
Are resolved easily

When you quiet the mind
You feel all is well regardless

UNDERSTAND YOUR SUFFERING...

If no matter what you achieve in your life
There is still a desire for more

If each desire once satisfied
Still leaves you empty inside

If the material world has lost its appeal
And you feel somewhat depressed

You are suffering from a spiritual thirst
That cannot be quenched by the world
But only by the spiritual dimension

It is your time to go within
Find the truth
Join your divine being
And return home

Suffering Comes From

Inability to deal with emotions
Ignorance of how the mind works
Inability to read situations properly

This is not a weakness - such fundamental things were not taught
Once you understand these things life becomes....

A joy despite and because of challenges
Peace becomes your natural state regardless
You find divine meaning to existence

Happiness

Self-Knowledge is seeing without judgment

Seeing that happiness
That is dependent
Is merely unhappiness woven in ignorance
Ignorance of once i have this i will be happy
Only to gain it and return to unhappiness and seeking again

Happiness dependent upon conditions remaining same
Is illusion
It is merely a comfort zone
Woven in fear
Leading to control and anxiety of change

True happiness is self-knowledge
Seeing through illusion
That happiness is your natural state
Not a dependent one

Can you see yet?

PAIN IS NATURAL

A response to the present moment
Training the being in wisdom, strength and depth
Adding to the richness of life and being
Passes easily with acceptance

Suffering is man-made
Created by resistance to present circumstances
Or dwelling on what has past
Accumulates with time
Rendering the being to weakness and sickness

Understanding is key
Letting go is vital

ALL ARE DIVINELY EQUAL

Only man and his ego places one man above another....

Every child is special, not just yours
Every prophet is equal to every man - only his stage in evolution
which separates him
Every life is important in the evolution of consciousness - not just
those that changed history
Every being is divine - behavior is not a measure of his being only
his consciousness

Me and mine is you trapped in ego - all is divinely one!

You Get What You Need

Life doesn't bring you what you want
It brings you what you need

When that is painful or challenging
It is only trying to free you from your own ignorance
It is mirroring you through your reactions

Stop blaming and justifying
And you will see and be free

Always ask 'what is life trying to teach me'?

INNER CONDITIONS CREATE
OR DESTROY HAPPINESS

You do not need to change the world
To be happy
You need to change how you see the world

Happiness is an internal experience created every moment
Not by outer circumstances
But by inner conditions

You are in control of your happiness
Once you learn to control your mind

What are you creating right now?

Belief Systems Are False

They are ideas without evidence

Their calling card is fear
Fear that essentially you know you do not know

Knowledge is seen directly
And thus requires no belief

Its calling card is authority
Authority which cannot be shaken

One will set you free from suffering
As only the realization of truth can

The other will keep you trapped
Offering only momentary release in the form of hope

Challenge your belief systems
Admit you do not know
Only then can the power of knowledge enter

Pain vs Suffering

When i finally came out of the darkness
I realized it was my greatest gift...

If you learn to understand suffering
Suffering comes to an end

If you learn to face pain
You will experience the utter joy of being alive

Suffering is in the mind - understand it
Pain is in the body - face it

Then you will know 'the peace that passeth all understanding'
(Philippians 4:7)

Endless Desire

As long as man seeks an orgasm
He will only ever be able to make sex, not love

This will only happen when man
Has outlived the pleasure principle
And thus seen the truth....

Pleasure is man's endless desire for fulfillment
Pleasure always leads to pain as emptiness returns
Pain of pleasure will eventually drive man to truth
Truth will take him home

His divine home is what he is searching for

HEART VS MIND

Follow your hearts calling -
Its nature is divine
Its intention is to serve you

Follow your mind
Its nature is fear
Its intention is to people please

Follow your heart
Its nature is love
Its intention is to bring you peace

Follow your mind
Its nature is conditioning
Its intention is empty pleasure

The calling of heart is silent 'knowing'
The calling of mind is obsessive noise

What is your heart saying?

LIVE YOUR DESIRES FULLY!

Guilt and regret serve only....

To suffocate the life in you
Preventing the seeing of truth and personal growth

Each desire is governed by the erroneous belief of fulfillment
Not until you have lived the desire fully can you see the truth
That is its divine purpose

Live each desire without guilt
You will see the truth and drop them
Eventually tiring of worldly desires
Seeking the only fulfillment, of the spiritual way

DEPRESSION

Depression is not cured by...

Adding worldly pleasures
Or by taking tablets

Depression is cured by...

Releasing the sadness of the past in you
And challenging negative thought patterns

LIVE AND LET LIVE

The true meaning of respect is to...
Live and let Live

Some may behave in one way
And you in another

Others may follow one religion
And you another or none

Live your own beliefs, that is your birth right
Let others live theirs, it is their birth right

Thus, live and let live
All else is control

You Are Perfect As You Are

Your flaws and imperfections were divinely created
They are the drive to take you home

We are each given a cross to carry
That serves as our resurrection to be reborn

Learn to accept yourself
And you will go home to your divine beautiful being

Learn to carry your cross
And you will transcend all suffering and be reborn into peace
and joy
You are a divine being living a human existence

THE REAL LAW OF ATTRACTION

What you play with in your mind
You create In your body
You manifest in your life

This is as real as it gets...

Understand the law
And you consciously create your life

Einstein Was Absolutely Correct!!

If you want peace - you must be at peace
If you want love - you must be love within
If you want abundance - you must feel rich already

You can only manifest conditions externally
That resonate with your energy internally

This is law of attraction, law of karma

PAIN IS NATURAL

Pain is not destructive
Unless you run from it

Then it becomes toxic to the body
And torturous to the mind

Face your pain
Feel its essence
And reveal the beauty that lies within

JUDGMENT IS DELUSIONAL

Judgment is the delusion of a mind
Looking to feel safe in an ever changing world

Judgment kills the mystery and beauty of life
As it kills the mystery and beauty of our true nature

You cannot judge that which constantly changes....

Allow each moment to rise
And each moment to pass

Only then will you know the truth of existence
And the true meaning of love

Self-Knowledge

The quality of your life is not determined by
Your external conditions
But by your internal conditions

To change your life
You must change your self

Self-Knowledge is the key to EVERYTHING!

THE REAL LAW OF KARMA

It's not about punishment
Its about freedom

Karma is your past conditioning
Attracting your present circumstances

Your present circumstances is...
Life trying to free you from the pain and ignorance of your past

It's called divine evolution

Law Of Attraction

Law of karma
Law of attraction
Are the same

It is not about punishment
It is about learning

Karma is your collected past manifesting as behavior
Attraction is your past manifesting as circumstances

Clear your karma
And you change what you attract

It's Not Personal

What someone does unto you
Is not PERSONAL

Harmful actions are always the result of ignorance and pain

What Someone does to you
They do to another
They do to themselves

The truth is...
If you do not understand and release your perpetrators
You become one of them

KNOW THY SELF...

It is the hardest task in existence
Thus few men have conquered it

Know thy self...

It is the hardest knowledge to obtain
But it is the only knowledge worth obtaining
Know thy self...

Without it Life is meaningless

YOU ARE COMPLETE

In being we are complete
In ego we are always lacking

Ego was needed as a child
But we're adults now

Destroy it and you will know freedom
Feed it and you will be imprisoned

As Within So Without

Your external conditions always resonate
With your own internal conditions

Thus......

If you are angry you will attract conflict situations
If you are at peace you will attract peaceful situations

Whatever you want externally
You need to be that internally, first

WHAT ARE YOU ATTRACTING?

The biggest delusion with the law of attraction
Is the idea that positive thinking creates what you want

Law of attraction works on the principle of
'As within so without'

What you believe
You feel
What you feel you create
You are creating every moment your next circumstances

YOU ARE HERE TO LEARN

You never made a mistake in your life
You are here to find the truth of existence

Falling is the process of learning

Judgment is your worst enemy
While acceptance is the key

PEACE

You cannot remain in peace with a mind that lives in....

The graveyard of the past
Or the fantasy of the future

Such a mind is always in conflict with reality

ACCEPTANCE OF SELF

Without acceptance of the self
You have no lasting...

Peace
Joy
Contentment

Without acceptance of the self
You are in conflict with...

Yourself
Others
Life

Without acceptance of the self
You have...

NOTHING!

KNOW HOW TO DIE

Only when you know how to live
Will you know how to die

Love life and you will love everything in it - including death

THE COURAGE TO BE HONEST

It's hard to be honest
In a world that doesn't like the truth

It takes great courage to be true
But without it you have nothing

Act from the heart and you'll always be true
Act from the mind and you'll be lucky to know the difference

No Such Thing As A Mistake

We are all here to learn

Your so called mistakes are that learning
So drop your guilt, anger and regret

You are doing the best you can

THIRST FOR TRUTH

There are many teachers
As there are paths

The teacher or path does not matter
Life will present what's right for you

The thirst for truth is all that is required
The rest is taken care of

It's a Journey not a path

THE DESTINATION

Jesus was the path for those in his time
Prophet Mohammed was the path for those his time
Buddha for those in his time

And still the above are the path for some in this time

As are....

Eckhart Tolle, Barry Long, Gandhi, Dali Lama, Anthony De'Mello, OSHO, and many more

Don't get stuck on the path
Stay focused on the destination

Truth Is Within You

There are many paths to truth...

Let your own heart guide you
Not those who claim to hold the only key

Truth is not bound by
One Book, One Teacher, One Culture, One Country

The language of truth is universal
And it is contained within your own heart

Learn to listen and trust 'the' laws of life

CLARITY IS THE KEY TO PEACE

Peace is not derived from external change
Peace is derived from the ability to see
First comes clarity then comes peace

Victim Of Mind

No one has hurt you more than your own mind...
Understand your mind or forever be its victim

What could be more important?

LET GO

Pain isn't harmful
Holding on to it is

Learn to let go
And pain will be your greatest gift

ENTER THE LIGHT

Don't worship a prophet - he is only a guide
Don't hold on to a book - it is only a map

You must enter the light by your OWN feet

Everything Is A Mirror...

Life is always trying to free you of your pain
By showing you your ignorance

Question is can you see?

IGNORANCE OF KNOWLEDGE

Many people have knowledge
Very few live it
The truth is most do not know how

Wisdom is knowledge lived

This Moment

The only certainty in your life is this moment

All fear, worry and anxiety is caused by trying to control the next
All regret, guilt and depression is caused by holding on to the last

Where do you live?

YOU ARE THE CREATOR
OF YOUR OWN DESTINY

Your thoughts create emotional vibrations
Your emotions attract situations that vibrate at the same frequency

As within so without
Understand your mind and you will understand your life

 64

Secret To Happiness...

Plan for the future but live in the present
Remember the past but dwell in the moment

Live by this law and peace will be your natural state

WITHIN YOU

Love starts within YOU
Not in a person

Peace begins in your MIND
Not in the World

God is known in your HEART
Not in a BOOK

This can only be found in the present moment

MAKE YOU OR BREAK YOU

Don't carry your problems
Face your challenges

One will break you
And one will make you

The choice is yours!

WE ARE PERFECT

You are already perfect
The only thing you need to change is your ignorance

For Example...

You can't try to be more patient
You can only understand impatience

Impatience is fighting with the present moment
Patience rises naturally when you accept and surrender

TIME TO EVOLVE

Stay in truth and awareness
And you will know joy and peace

Stay in ignorance
And you will know suffering and confusion

Every situation and person
Only shows you your own internal state

Its life trying to help you evolve

Man And Religion

Jesus did not teach violence as Christianity does not kill
Only man in his ignorance does this

Prophet Mohammed did not teach violence as Islam does not kill
Only man in his ignorance does this

Religion does not harm
But man in his ignorance will use it so

Until man evolves out of this stage of ignorance
He will destroy everything he touches

We are at that stage now
Man is finally understanding his ignorance

REALITY IS DISTORTED

When mind and pain interact
Reality becomes distorted

The deeper the pain
The greater the distortion

Sit with pain
And quiet the mind

SELF-WORTH

Self-worth is not destroyed by others
It is destroyed by you!

Its comes naturally when you stop condemning yourself
And allowing yourself to be condemned

Thus know...

You are doing the best you can
And that is good enough

Society is insane
So don't measure yourself by it!

KNOW YOUR MIND!

Depression and anger is a mind stuck in the past
Anxiety and fear is a mind stuck in the future

Peace and contentment is a mind at rest in this moment

Where is your mind?

Empty Inside

Do you feel empty inside?
That life has little meaning?

No matter what you get or achieve
You still feel a sense of lack?

Is this all there is?

NO!!!
You are just looking in the wrong place!

The Delusion Of Love

Love is the most powerful force in the universe
But 'self-love' is delusional

There is no separate self to love
There is only YOU

What you seek is already within you
It is the feeling of love

It rises naturally with knowledge
And acceptance of who you REALLY are - LIFE

UNCONDITIONAL LOVE....

It doesn't matter where it comes from
It is the most powerful force on earth

It is God In Existence!

Remember to express yours!

WHAT WILL YOU CREATE TODAY?

Think angry thoughts
Create angry emotions

By the law of cause and effect
You will attract destructive situations

Know your mind and it will be your best friend
Remain in ignorance and it will be your worst enemy

LEARN YOUR LESSONS

Don't pray for things to be different
Pray to know why they are here

The sooner you know the lesson
The sooner difficulties disappear

The objective of life
Is to evolve to a higher state

This will be done with you kicking or screaming
Or dancing and singing

Freedom From Suffering!

Accept pain when it rises
Learn to let go
And it will set you free

Accept challenges when they come
Learn your lessons
And they will set you free

YOU GET WHAT YOU NEED

Do not worry about the future
Or pray for future riches

You can only receive...
That which is necessary for your growth

Be still and await its arrival
Enjoy the mystery and perfection of life

QUITE SIMPLY...

The key to happiness lies in the knowledge of mind
The key to unhappiness lies in ignorance of mind

Quite simply...

Your mind is the greatest tool in existence
Or the most destructive force in nature

Please tell me what is more important than self-knowledge?

THE LIGHT

The world is a dark place without
The light of spirit....

And the spirit is within you

ENEMIES – LET THEM GO

Understand your enemies
Don't hate them

That sets you free
Not them

They remain a prisoner
Of their own tortuous self

BE TRUE

Be true to yourself
And to all others you are true

Go against yourself
And to all others you lie

People pleasing is just a lack of self-worth
But people pleasing also destroys self-worth

Learn how to value yourself

DO YOU WANT PEACE?

You say you want peace?
Every time you resist a situation

You create conflict
Every time you judge another person

You create conflict
Ignorance is the primary cause of all suffering

PAIN VS SUFFERING

Pain is now
Suffering is past or future

Pain felt and expressed now
Transforms into wisdom and peace later

Pain resisted and repressed now
Turns into ignorance and suffering later

Run from pain
And suffering will be your constant companion

Self-Knowledge

Know thy self
And you will know joy and peace

Stay in ignorance
And you know suffering and confusion

Every situation and person
Only shows you your own internal state

Its only life trying to help you evolve

KNOW THEY SELF OR SUFFER

Emotion....
Anger is past pain unexpressed
Depression is past sadness repressed

Mind:
Guilt and anger is a mind living in the past
Worry and anxiety is a mind dwelling in the future

Self-knowledge makes life worth living
Without it you suffer...

Ignorance Destroys Health

Health and wellness is not achieved
By right nutrition
Or by right exercise...

It is achieved by knowing why
You are not doing them...

A healthy mind looks after the body instinctively...

KNOWLEDGE OF THE HEART

Listen to your heart
It knows what the mind does not

Listen to the heart
It knows what's right for you

Listen to the heart
It knows it's time for change

Listen to the heart
It will get you through

Listen to the heart
And all will be well

Your task? Is to know its calling card!

REPRESSION IS REGRESSION

Repressed pain will destroy your health
And your life...

Face your pain
And well-being will be your constant companion

Run from pain
And suffering will be your constant shadow

ESSENCE OF GOD

To feel the presence of God as a living reality
You must learn to quiet the mind
And stop creating emotional turmoil

The essence of God is felt in the stillness within

LOVE IS NOW

Dwell in the past and you will repeat it
Dwell in the future and you will fear it
Dwell in the present and you will love it

HEALTHY MIND
HEALTHY BODY

Negative thoughts create negative energy
Negative energy damages the body

This is fact not fiction!

Understand the mind and you stop this cycle
Understand the mind and you create health and wellness

LISTEN...

A person of substance...

Is a person who listens to the heart
And has the courage to follow

Listen to others
But follow your own heart
Your heart knows what's right for you!

BE TRUE TO YOURSELF

Say what you think
Mean what you say
And do what you say and think

Be yourself, in reality that's all you have!

DREAMS OF THE HEART

Use the mind to create the dreams of your heart
Let the mind use you and it will destroy them

The mind is a wonderful tool
But a terrible master

Understand the mind and you become the master of your life!
Ignorance of mind and you become its slave

PERCEPTION IS THE KEY

The difference between happiness and unhappiness is perception!

Understanding the mind is a necessity for all
Not a privilege for the few

WELLNESS IS YOUR ESSENCE

At The heart of every desire is the desire for wellness

It is never the object of desire you really want
It is always the feeling associated with the desire
The feeling of happiness/wellness

You don't have to be someone or obtain something to get it...
You can naturally create it yourself

It is the essence of your true nature

NOTHING OF VALUE
IS JUST GIVEN

Fight for what you want
At least you know if you don't get it
It wasn't because you didn't try
It was because it wasn't right....

Not only will you sleep at night
But something better will be in sight

 100

LIFE IS SIMPLE

If someone is genuine
It is evident in their behavior before their words

If a situation is right for you
It is evident in your heart before your mind

If there is confusion....
Something is wrong

ARE YOU TRUE?

Your words do not define you
Your behavior does

Saying you care
Without showing you care is false

HOW TO GIVE

If charity begins at home....
Remember the world is your home

A warm smile
A kind gesture
Sometimes that's all it takes to remind someone life is good.

YOU GET WHAT YOU ARE

If you want love
Be that love first

You attract according to your energy
Not according to your desire

TO BE TRULY HAPPY

You must go into the storms of life
Instead of running from them.

The storms come disguised as challenges
But therein lies your fears

Therein lies yourself....
The parts that scare you

Go into the storm
Face yourself
And leave your fear behind

WHAT IS YOUR GUT SAYING?

Use the mind for tasks
The emotions to express your experiences
Your gut to tell you the truth

If the silence inside you speaks - listen carefully!

POWER OF SELF-ACCEPTANCE

Until you accept yourself internally
Nothing can really change externally

Suicide Isn't Selfish

It is selfless!

Quite often the person feels their own suffering
has become a burden for those closet to them.

Thus, ending their own pain is also ending pain for
others - in the long run!

To get over a suicide, you must understand!
To prevent suicide, we All must learn how to deal with pain.

YOU GET YOUR ENERGY
NOT YOUR DESIRE

You are not your behavior
You are your intentions....

Thus, if you want to see good
Be that good
Not in your words
But in your heart

If you want love
Be that love
Not in your selfish needs
But in your heart

You can't get what you wish for
You can only get what you create....

No More Pain!!

People commit suicide....
Not because they don't want to live
But because they don't want to feel....

For the family - without understanding there is no healing.

LIFE IS AS IT IS

Life is as it is
See that
Live that

And all fear disappears

HAPPINESS VS UNHAPPINESS
IS PERCEPTION ONLY

Life is Difficult
But it is Good

How you experience it
Depends on your perception

LEARN TO RIDE THE WAVE

Life challenges never end
And Pain is inevitable

But....

As you learn to ride the wave of life
Challenges become gifts of growth
And pain just another energy field

Don't be afraid of life
Live all aspects of it to the full

Cyber World Is
Killing The World

It's the latest addiction
An escapism from reality

It kills your ability to feel life
The needs of people
The beauty of nature
The joy of living

It's turning you into a zombie
Killing your relationships
And poisoning your children

Wake up and start living again before you forget how.

FROM ONE GOOD WOMAN TO ANOTHER

Don't waste your time with boys....
Know your worth
And settle for nothing less

Eventually a man will come along
And reflect that worth

CRYING IS THE ANECDOTE
TO SUFFERING

The only way to dissolve pain
Is to cry it away

Then Let Go!

LEARN TO LET GO!

Don't hold on
To those that no longer belong

Feel the pain of departure
But cherish the love ever after

Love is a gift
However long it lasts!

End Of Suffering

It's OK not to be OK!

When you let pain be....
It disappears!

It's only trapped energy!

Are You Looking For God?

God is life itself!

That is why scientists cannot find a beginning
And there is no end, only transformation of form

There is no separate divine being
You and everything around you
Is that which you seek

The meaning of man's existence....
Is to realize that

THE GREATEST GIFT

Is to know, finally
That you know nothing

In that acceptance
Is the deep peace you search for

Life Doesn't Get Easier!

You just get stronger....

If you choose

Happiness is feeling alive!

All you really want is to feel alive again
But first you must come alive again....

Do you even know how?

THE ART OF GIVING

Find your passion
And you will find your joy

Find your joy
And you will find your love

Find your love....
And you will be love

Be Love
And you will give love

ARE YOU HAPPY?

Happiness is a state of mind
Not a state of circumstances

HOW DO YOU SHOW
THAT YOU LOVE?

You don't need anything
To give everything....

Love can be expressed in a million simple ways.

DO YOU REALLY LOVE?

Kindness in words create 'trust'
Kindness in thought create 'good intention'
But only kindness in action shows the strength of your love

It's Not Enough To Say 'I Love You'

BEING STRAIGHT ISN'T RUDE, ITS A GIFT!

What you repress
Will possess you...

Moods will arise
Destroy the good
Within you
And around you

If someone upsets you
Have the courage to tell them

Learn to be straight
And life will be great!

You Have Everything You Are Looking For

All everyone truly wants is to
Feel Alive Again

When you feel alive....
You naturally feel good
You are in love with life
You are filled with Joy
You are so very grateful

You Are Happy!

Be still
Feel the goodness of life within
You are everything you have been searching for

STOP SEARCHING

You cannot find happiness
While you are searching for it....

You Are It!

ARE YOU REALLY A SEEKER OF TRUTH?

Truth that is not found in your own experience
Is not the truth...

It is either someone else's truth
Or it is a lie

For truth to really set you free
You must be the one to discover it

Happiness Is Within
Not Without

Are you lonely
And always need company?

Do you constantly cover up the silence
With TV/Radio and Facebook?

Do you need extra stimulation
From Cigarettes, Alcohol, Drugs, Food and Sex?

Then you cannot find happiness....
Because you are constantly running from it.

Face loneliness, go into the silence, seek contentment in now
And happiness will follow....
It is your natural state

WHY WORRY?

Don't ruin today
With the worry of tomorrow

Tomorrow, it may not even matter

THE LAW OF LOVE

Love doesn't die
Because it was a lie

Love died because you failed
To nurture it

Love is the strongest force in the universe
But without feeding it....
It cannot survive

Pray the Right Way
- For Gods Sakes!

Don't pray for peace in the world
Pray for peace in your own heart

We have all contributed to the violence
In this world
By being ignorant to the violence
In ourselves

Be at peace and you will teach peace
That is the only way to save the world

THE WISDOM TO KNOW
THE DIFFERENCE

Love is withstanding the pain of others
For the greater good

Wisdom is seeing when
There is no greater good

RELIGION AND GOD AREN'T NECESSARY

Only a pure heart is!

Religion and God cannot give you this
Only a logical mind can

Learn to see correctly
And Love will follow

True Freedom

Being around family and friends is definitely beautiful
But learning to enjoy being alone is a true gift

It's all to do with how you think...

LOVE IS MORE IMPORTANT THAN OPINIONS

Don't let the need to be right
Destroy your need to love

Keep love in your heart
And differences will be like sugar and spice
'All things are nice'

PUT LOVE FIRST

Then Everything Else Will Work Out!

Be The Love You Want To Receive

A smile
A kind word
A simple hello

Acts of love can be given every day
They cost nothing
But they mean everything....

THE TRUTH IS HARD
BUT IT'S WORTH IT

It is the highest form of respect
To simply tell someone the truth

Telling lies is not only cowardly
It is also very hurtful

Are You The Problem?

When a situation keeps repeating itself
It is usually because you haven't learnt yet

Be honest with yourself!

MY TRUTH!

What I learnt....

I am not optimistic
Neither am I positive
And i do not believe in hope

I just know...
Everything is ok, regardless!

MINE IS THE BEST

Why do some religious people reject...
Other Religions
Other Teachers
Other Paths
Or Claim 'mine is the best'?

Simply, because to make such claims
Makes them feel like they are a part of 'The Elite'
The Elite therefore makes them 'Special'
And being special gives them 'Self-Worth'

Insecurity is the cause of arrogance
And extremist views and behavior

The deeper the insecurity....
The greater the ignorance
The more destructive the behavior

TRULY LISTENING IS
TRULY LOVING

Bloody Ego....

It is one of the hardest ego traits to transcend
But WHEN I do
Truly I will know, I am closer to God!

FINDING THE TRUTH

You don't have to follow religion
Believe in God
Or seek a spiritual path

Your life itself is the only path
And you have no choice but to follow it

WHO ARE YOU?

Man of truth...
Will be true to his character in all things
Whilst forsaking his reputation

This Doesn't Take Courage, Simply....

A Man who is sincere
Would rather die
Than be fake

Don't Be Fooled!

The difference between Knowing God
And Believing in God....

Is in your behavior!

DO YOU HAVE THE COURAGE TO BE HONEST?

While your self-worth depends on public opinion
You will always be dishonest and fake.

You may justify this by claiming you are....
Serving them by
Protecting their feelings
But this isn't true, is it?

Really, you are serving yourself
And your need to be liked.

BEING YOURSELF - IS THE
HIGHEST FORM OF SELF LOVE

Speak your mind
Express your feelings

Simply, be true to yourself
And you are true to all others

People pleasing
Is self-denying
Fake
And totally dishonest to all

Being true
Is self-cleansing
Self-healing
Self-loving
And totally just to all

Do you love yourself and others enough to be true?

THE MOST IMPORTANT RELATIONSHIP

As Within So Without....

As you treat yourself
So to all others will treat you

The most important relationship in your life
Is thus with yourself

A Woman's Worth....

Gone are the days when
Being respected, treated fairly and equally
Is considered 'Good Treatment' by a man

Now It is your right!

If a man truly loves you
He will show you
In every way, every day!

Not with money
But with his heart
In the small things he does
Not just the things he says

Know your worth woman
And then settle for nothing less

RELATIONSHIP POISON

No relationship can survive
The destructive force of arrogance

Do you love your arrogance more than your relationship?

THE POWER OF YOUR LOVE

When you believe in your love
You will believe in the impossible

There is nothing you won't do

GREAT DREAMS REQUIRE
SMALL STEPS

All dreams are achievable
No matter how impossible it seems

All you have to do is believe
Stay calm
And do your role

Take the steps you can take today
And the steps you can do tomorrow

Face the challenges as they arise
Get up when you fall
And know that all great things never come easy

One step at a time

BEAUTY OF CHANGE

The sky is always changing
In that lies it beauty

Your life is always changing
In that lies it's mystery

Don't hold on to the old
Or the beauty of the new cannot be seen

Life changes because that it is life
But also because it is what you need

Thus, let go of the old
And welcome the new
Enjoy the mystery it holds for you

Fight For Your Dreams

If you want something bad enough
You must be willing to fight hard enough

God Loves A Trier....

That means you must do your part
Until there is nothing left to do...

Then wait in utter amazement as the world opens up for you
Either you get what you fought for

Or something much better

Fight for your dreams!

WE ARE ALL ONE

You didn't build your country - so it's not YOURS
You didn't create your religion - so it's not YOURs

To claim it's MY country and MY religion
Only creates SEPARATION and VIOLENCE

The ego uses it to increase its sense of superiority
And perceived sense of power

In TRUTH we are all ONE
Regardless of what religion we follow
Or land we were born in

God created us EQUAL

TRUTH

There is only ONE truth
It is NOW

All else is a lie

THE ONLY FIGHT
WORTH FIGHTING

Don't worry too much about the ways of people
Say your piece according to your energy
But don't waste your energy fighting them

Don't worry too much about the ways of society
Do your piece as your energy dictates
But don't waste your energy obsessing

Your purpose is to know yourself
And overcome Your ignorance
Society and People are there for that purpose
Fighting them is missing the point
Learn from them and you are living your life purpose

What are your circumstances trying to teach you?

Don't take it seriously

The world and all its drama
Is all manifestations of unconsciousness
Expressing itself in the play of form
Don't take it seriously; its not real

Your mind is made up of conditioning
Manifesting as circumstances
It is but your karmic past, not reality
Don't take it seriously; its not real

The only way out of illusion
Is to find your spirit
And live there

Play with the world
But don't take it too seriously

WHERE RELIGION
GOES WRONG

When you take religion as a part of your identity

You become offended, hurt and aggressive
If anyone questions your religion
Because, you take it as a personal attack on you
Rather than a difference of opinion

You destroy peace, love and above all - God
You create war

Religion is no more than a method
That some may choose
To get close to God

It is not sacred
If it were, billions of people would be peaceful beings by now
It is only a method that can help
But only those that are ready

Those that are ready
Can use any method, or no method
Because they see their very life is the method

If you are truly following Religion to find God
Then Love should be in your heart always
When love turns to anger
Now you know it's your ego identity you are pleasing
Not God

Suffering or Joy
- You Choose

My childhood taught me suffering
My suffering taught me wisdom
My wisdom taught me...

I have a choice!

Focus my mind on negative things
And i will experience suffering
Focus my mind on positive things
And i will experience joy

What's the point of anything if we don't get that right?

Why do I suffer?

The world is empty
And the world is cruel
Look for happiness in it and you will suffer

Man must go deep within himself
Through all the layers of pain and conditioning
And past the torturous mind

Only then will you know happiness
And only then will you find the reason for existing

We have reached that time now

WHY SUICIDE?

People who take their own life...
Aren't weak
Aren't selfish
Aren't necessarily atheist

They are tired of suffering
And see no way out

Many factors contribute to that moment
Not just one event

I was there once upon a time
My partner took his life
And many friends

No one is to blame
It's just a way out for some
And another way to die

You can't trust man

You can't trust your parents won't damage you
You can't your friends won't hurt you
You can't trust your child won't desert you
And you can't trust your true love won't leave you

The ONLY thing you can really trust
Is what happens is right for you

You haven't learnt yet!

Situations are meant to make you grow....

A good sign you haven't learnt your lesson
Is when the situation keeps repeating itself

Learn your lesson
And the situation will end

A simple law of life

DON'T BE OFFENDED

Before you get offended by someone's words
Just remember maybe you were meant to hear them

Before you get hurt by someone's behavior
Just remember maybe you were meant to feel that

Every situation is there to teach you
You attracted it for a reason

Remember that and you'll learn quickly
You may feel pain
But you will not suffer

ARE YOU ESCAPING?

Most of your deepest desires
Are just a means to escape this moment

A BETTER WORLD
STARTS WITH YOU

The laws of life are simple
Made plain and clear

They are the only solution
To world in total despair

Man must apply them to himself at first
And see his problems disappear
Only then can you have world leaders
That rule with a divine spear

So, man sit with yourself this moment
Feel the life within
Pay attention to the stillness
The laws of life there in

Pain is Your Purification

Pain comes to purify your heart
So that you may feel the light of God
Even in the darkest of places

So please don't cry for my pain
Or try to offer me solutions
Know that I rejoice inside
As God beacons me closer

One day my tears will be that of joy
My pain a thing of the past
The light of God is ever closer
Burning the darkness from my heart

THE WAY OUT IS THE WAY IN

We all have re-occurring painful emotions
Depression
Fear
Insecurity
Low self-worth

Most of us have tried....
Counselling
Drinking
Medication
Drugs
Over eating

Anything to escape
But most have failed

Why?
Pain is old energy that needs to be actively dissolved
The only way out of it is to go into it

Sit with it, feel it, allow it, don't think of it and it will dissolve
layer by layer.

PROTECT THE TRUTH

Let me ask you this....

If Jesus, Prophet Mohamed and Buddha
Got high on drugs and alcohol
Didn't respect their body or environment
Treated animals cruelly
Neglected those in need
Only loved their family and friends
People pleased rather than stand up for the truth

Would you follow them?

Then why do you 'Like' posts from spiritual hypocrites?
Those that preach the truth but don't live it.

Religious preachers destroyed the word 'God' with their divine
words but barbaric behavior...

Don't let spiritual hypocrites destroy our sacred truths also

HARDSHIPS

Being good....
Doesn't prevent hardships
Doesn't stop your loved ones dying young
Your greatest love leaving you
Losing all your possessions

No use praying to keep all you love
Telling God how good you are

God knows the greatest saint was once the greatest sinner
And the greatest sinner will rise to be the greatest saint
That's the process of evolution
And all are equal under it

Hardships are part of life
And often your greatest gift
They teach you that which the world cannot...

Truth, wisdom, courage, peace, joy and God
All these reside within the soul
Being occupied with the world however
You forget to look there

Dark Night of the Soul

Sometimes I don't know what to do
Sometimes I haven't even one clue
Sometimes all I have is you

Sometimes you are louder than the church bells
Sometimes quieter than a mouse
Sometimes I cannot find you
All alone in this old empty house

Sometimes I scream in frustration
Sometimes I cry in pain
Sometimes all is overwhelming
Sometimes I feel insane

Then I'm reminded to sit, my child
Be still in mind and emotion
Stop creating such commotion
Im always here beside you

I am the beauty in the stars
The compelling-nous of the moon
I am the peace you feel in silence
And joy that always comes soon

I am beside you
Within you
Outside you….

Divine Soul - I am you!

Love - the most misused word in history!

Do you know what love is?

Love is giving to another when they need it most
Love is giving to another even when you don't like them
Love is giving to another even when they don't like you
Love is telling another the truth even when you will be condemned
Love is not about being there all the time, it is about being there when it counts
Love is giving without expecting gratitude
Love is giving without getting 'anything' in return
Love is not confined to family and friends, where you are always getting back a return
Love is giving to a stranger, an animal, plants and even to your enemy

Love has to be present within you every minute of the day, ready to express itself when the moment requires

Love is giving because quite simply...you have no choice

Now ask yourself the question - Do I Love?

LIVE YOUR OWN LIFE

Most of what you see around you is delusional
Most of the 'happy' people are in fact suffering
Most of the social systems are corrupt
Most religions are contaminated

Don't live your life according to what you see

Listen to your heart to know what you want
Use the logic of your mind to create it
Then be patient and see if it's your destiny

Listen to your heart to know what is right
Use the logic of the mind to implement it
Then watch as life teaches you

All you need to know is within you
But you don't know how to listen - start now!

LIFE ISN'T COMPLICATED; WE ARE!

Life is simple
But it's hard

We make it complicated
Because we expect it to be easy

Understand the nature of life
And you will understand the nature of your problems
They make your life rich
And give you depth

Without them you can't grow

TRUST LIFE NOT PEOPLE

'Love is giving
Someone the power to destroy you
But trusting them not too' - Wrong!!

Love is giving
Someone the power to destroy you
But trusting life to decide

Sometimes you need a kick up the arse
Rather than a helping hand
Only life knows which

Remember...Your greatest lessons often come
In your greatest pains

WALK THE WALK

Or shut up!

There are too many fakes in the world....

Spiritual Teachers
Religious Preachers
Therapist Healers

People that talk the talk
But don't walk the walk

Don't be one of them!

Speak your truth, only
That which you live,
Anything else is false

TRUE LOVE

Love is not in your words
It is in your behavior

When you love....

There isn't a mountain too high to climb
Water too deep to cross
Distance too far to travel
An Obstacle too hard to over come

When you love....

Behavior is the proof
Words are just an expression

How much do you show you love?

 181

TRUST IS ALL I HAVE

Sometimes it's so hard
Sometimes the road isn't clear
Sometimes I wonder what lies ahead
Sometimes I just cry in frustration

But all the time I know....
Everything is as it should be
And I will always get what is right for me

Sometimes all you have left is Trust

 182

HAVE COMPASSION

Whatever flaws you have
Don't condemn yourself
Have compassion....

You did not choose ignorance
It chose you....

The purpose of existence is to dissolve ignorance
And find the truth
To dissolve pain
And create peace
To dissolve darkness
And free the light

To do this we must carry ignorance
To see the truth of it
And set it free

The journey is tough
Have compassion
And then do your part

The journey is tough
Have compassion
And then do your part

HEALTHY LOVE

People who play mind games
Do so to gain control
To feel secure
To take the power

But in the end, you lose that which you are so desperately trying
to keep.

True love is precious and needs to be treated as such
It requires vulnerability
Honesty
And openness to change

True love is very rare
So when it comes take good care

Love - Misery or Joy?

While you need what you love
For self-worth and to give your life meaning
You will be forever insecure, fearful and miserable.

While you need what you love
You will harm and destroy

A parent that needs their child to create meaning
Will over medicate in times of sickness through fear of loss
Will prevent them from exploring their environment and stump
their growth
Will find emptiness and pain when they become independent
from them

A partner who needs another to fill the void
Will seek control and possession of the other
Will live in fear of losing them
Will find little solace without them

We don't need to find love
We are the essence of love
When you find the source within you
All fear and misery disappear
And your love for another will be true and serving

To love only the human way
You will remain afraid and insecure
And your love will one-minute serve
And the next destroy

Look within for love
And without you will be surrounded by it

 185

No Law, No Religion - Only Purification Needed

Man, who purifies his mind
Releases his past pain
And dissolves his conditioning

Needs no law or religion
To tell him what's right or wrong
Purified - he feels connected to all things
Now harming anything is like harming himself

Law and religion are only necessary
To control man who hasn't evolved to that state yet

Truth and where to find it

Truth cannot be taught
Only knowledge can

Knowledge lived, is truth
Therefore, only YOU can find it

You must walk the walk
To talk the talk
That's the truth

Bloody Pain - When Will It End?

Let me tell you a secret - It Doesn't!!
But let me tell you another secret - It Doesn't Matter!

These things your Psychologist and Psychiatrist don't tell you
because they don't know!

Pain whatever it is....
Depression
Anxiety
Destructive habits
Insecurity
Anger
Fear
Low self-worth
Etc. etc...

Once you understand them,
stop feeding them
and allow them to be,
they dissolve....

And You Evolve!

JUDGEMENT

Each time you judge
You fail to see....
The joy, the love and peace
Of just ME

I am life
Within and without
I am life
Truth, love and alive

Judgement kills
All that really is
Creating delusion
Suffering and pain

Relax the mind
Allow this moment to be
And see truly what is
The beauty in ME

PAVE THE WAY FOR OTHERS

There is only truth and ignorance....

One creates conflict and violence and destroys love
The other creates peace and joy and is love itself

If you are a seeker of truth you are contributing to peace
If you stay in ignorance you are contributing to conflict

Truth is the true seeing of oneself without judgement

Genuine Love

All without fail seek genuine love
That soothes your heart and warms your soul

All without fail find the pretenders
That leave your heart empty and insecure

Dress to impress
Put on your heirs and graces
And speak of status and fame

You will attract the love of pretenders

Be yourself
Speak your mind
And serve rather than gain

You will attract the love
That will serve and sooth your pain

These are the lessons we are here to learn
These are the Laws of Life

TRUE LOVE

Having it all in one person is what is meant by 'Soul Partner'

But it is not about 'Luck'
It is about not settling for less

Everyone has someone that is truly 'right' for them
But you have to be ready first
And that may require time

When you find that person
You will know....
There will be no choice

You will be compelled to love
Despite the complaints of the mind
You will be compelled to love
Despite the doubts of the people

You will be compelled to love
Because this time it is true

PAINS OF LIFE

Accept the pains of life as you accept joy
It pushes you deeper, higher and purifies you
It is here to serve you,

But be aware of continued suffering in your life....
It is life trying to teach you something
But you aren't listening,

Pain passes and makes you feel alive
Suffering lingers and makes you miserable

Learn to know the difference....

Mind Games

Dwell in the past and you create....
Regret, Guilt, Anger and Depression
This will be how you experience TODAY

Dwell in the future and you create....
Frustration, Fear, Anxiety and Worry
This will be how you experience TODAY

Let go of past and future - you create....
Peace, Joy and Contentment

If you play with the mind; it will play with you!

GOING ROUND IN CIRCLES

The triggers change....

The person, place and situation
But....

The same pain arises
The same thoughts accompany
The same behavior responds

You are trapped in your conditioning and past pain
You are experiencing Deja Vu

Until you learn how to dissolve the past in you
You will just keep going around in circles

WHAT IS TRUTH?

Seek the truth,
Live the truth
Be the truth

The truth is being true to yourself each moment....
by, being your self

The truth is seeking to understand yourself each moment
by, facing your dark side

The truth is the only 'real' freedom there is....
but you must Live it to be liberated by it

True Partners

Don't withdraw when the other is down
Don't say I love you without actions
Don't leave the other carrying most of the weight

True Partners....

Support each other when times are hard
Show Love through actions first
Give everything they have

True partnership is rare, but don't settle for anything less

Being Straight Means I Don't Hate??

Hatred, anger, being fake....
All comes from not being straight

Speak your mind
Express your emotions
Be honest about your perceptions

No matter the consequences
Being straight clears your mind
And cleans your emotions
Allows people to trust you

Hiding the truth
Creates destructive emotions
Wrong perceptions
Fake behavior
And mistrust

Being straight takes courage
But it is the true meaning of freedom and honesty

HEALING IS A PROCESS....

Each have our pain
Each have our ignorance
And each have our healing proccss

Working as a therapist and public speaker for 10 years
I realize there are no conclusions to reach, there
are only steps to take up an endless ladder.

Never give up climbing that ladder maybe you will reach the end
of your pain or maybe you won't, who knows?
But what i do know, is that you will reach the light and that was
the point!

Healing Is A Process - A climb to the light!

LIFE IS GROWTH

Life Isn't about....
How much money you earned
How high up the career ladder you climbed
How educated you are
What country you were born In
What you look like
Or Even How Good or Bad You Supposedly Are

Life Is about how much you grew whilst you were engaged In those things

Life Is about learning not accumulating

In that we are all equal
And we all have the same chances

In that life Is just

TRUST

You never know what's truly coming
Even when you think you do

But a truly spiritual being knows....

What joins me on my path today
Come good, mad, sad or bad

Is exactly what i need right now
That will eventually make me truly glad

LISTEN

Don't look for permanence in anything
Look for teachings
You never know when new things begin
And when they will end

As it is said in the Muslim Religion
'Life is not a rest, it is a test'

Enjoy your joys
And welcome your challenges

Always remind yourself of the bigger picture...
You are here to Learn and to Love
If you are doing that you are on the right track

BE TRUE

In a world of contradictions
And confusion
All you have is truth

Speak your truth
Live your truth regardless

On your death bed you will not regret
Being courages enough to speak the truth
But you will regret all the times you are too afraid
To be honest

Don't forsake yourself
For the sake of pleasing others

Be true
It's all you have

 203

GOD IS NOT IN A BOOK

God is in your life

God's word has been recorded in many books
But you must not worship a book
It is only a map

Your divine task is to find God as a living reality
Then God is in your heart
And no book is needed

I LOVE YOU

The misused and misunderstood word in history

The only true measure
Is your actions
Not your words

Don't Be Fooled Again

LIFE IS TOUGH

Sometimes you know not why you suffer
Sometimes you know not why you exist
Sometimes you no not how to continue
In those times all I know Is God
In those times that Is all I need

I suffered all my life with only respites in between
But suffering brought me to my knees
And when I looked up I saw God
That Is all I see now...

Suffering was my gift

KNOW A MAN BY HIS ACTIONS NOT HIS WORDS...

Man calls himself religious
And kills in the name of it
Actions speak louder than words

Man loves his family
And thinks he Is good
Such love Is instinctive (unless disturbed)
Not a measure of a good heart

Man that cannot harm any living creature
With or without religion
Is truly a divine man

Man that loves all living things
People, animals and plants
Not just his own circle
Is truly a man of pure heart

What kind of man are you?

YOUR CHILDREN

Are not your children
They belong to life

Serve them
But don't live for them

You have your own journey to take
They are apart of it
But not the essence of it

They have their journey to take
You are apart of it
But not the essence of it

All children are your children
Learn to love equally
Only then is your love serving life
Rather than just serving you

What kind of love do you have?

Religion Doesn't Make You Good!

After living in a religion dominated country I observed:

Religion doesn't lead you to God
And religion doesn't purify you
Practicing what you preach leads you to God
And practicing what you preach purifies you

When you are ready all paths and all methods lead you to God
When you are ready you don't need any path or any method
When you are ready the truth becomes your destiny

Follow religion because it comes from the heart
Not because you are afraid of hell

A true religion should set you free
Not in-prison you in fear

I love all religions, all messengers, teachers, prophets,
But, I only follow God!

HOW TRUE IS YOUR LOVE?

When you truly love...
You make time
You notice
You listen
You speak
You fight

When you truly love you can't help but give
When you don't, you have to make the effort

When you truly love you give OF yourself
When you don't, you give TO yourself

Be honest and ask yourself - do you truly love?

WORDS FROM BEYOND

I had a dream that I was free....
So life said, 'then you must see'

I had a dream that I Could feel....
So life said, 'then you heal'

I had a dream that I was alive....
So life said, 'then you must survive.

You must survive
You must survive

You must survive the dream my friend....
Most die before they wake.

I had a dream
No....
You are the dream